DON'T FUMBLE
YOUR RETIREMENT

NEW MONEY LESSONS LEARNED BY
FOUR-TIME SUPER BOWL CHAMPION ROCKY BLEIER

DON'T FUMBLE
YOUR RETIREMENT

NEW MONEY LESSONS LEARNED BY
FOUR-TIME SUPER BOWL CHAMPION ROCKY BLEIER

Published by Advantage, Charleston, South Carolina.
Member of Advantage Media Group.

ADVANTAGE is a registered trademark and the Advantage colophon is a trademark of Advantage Media Group, Inc.

Printed in the United States of America.

ISBN: 978-159932-290-2
LCCN: 2011939446

This publication is designed to provide accurate and authoritative information in regard to the subject matter covered. It is sold with the understanding that the publisher is not engaged in rendering legal, accounting, or other professional services. If legal advice or other expert assistance is required, the services of a competent professional person should be sought.

Advantage Media Group is proud to be a part of the Tree Neutral® program. Tree Neutral offsets the number of trees consumed in the production and printing of this book by taking proactive steps such as planting trees in direct proportion to the number of trees used to print books. To learn more about Tree Neutral, please visit **www.treeneutral.com**. To learn more about Advantage's commitment to being a responsible steward of the environment, please visit **www.advantagefamily.com/green**

Advantage Media Group is a leading publisher of business, motivation, and self-help authors. Do you have a manuscript or book idea that you would like to have considered for publication? Please visit **www.amgbook.com** or call **1.866.775.1696**

Dedicated to the wonderful people who choose to live, work, raise their families and retire in western Pennsylvania.

I dedicate this book to us.

 **ROCKY BLEIER'S** life story – a gripping tale of courage on both the football fields of America and the battlefields of Vietnam – has held audiences in rapt attention for years. As he enters a new arena, retirement income planning, Rocky addresses many of the daunting issues facing retirees today. Sharing new money lessons he has learned while planning his own retirement, Rocky demonstrates the same optimism, sense of humor and steadfast determination that were his trademarks as a Pittsburgh Steelers running back.

Lacking the ideal "build" of a running back, Rocky had to run harder and play smarter to be able to stand out. Despite his drive and ability to make the big play, the Pittsburgh Steelers only considered him a late round pick in 1968. But before the season ended that first year, he was drafted again, this time by the United States Army.

At the height of the Vietnam War, Rocky was thrust into combat early and was seriously wounded when his platoon ran into an ambush. Receiving wounds from both rifle fire and grenade fragments in his legs, he was barely able to walk and his professional football career seemed to have ended before it began.

For more than two years, he drove himself. Little by little he overcame obstacles and fought his way back.

Rocky not only made the Pittsburgh Steelers again in 1971, but also eventually became a starting running back on a team that won four Super Bowls and became the greatest football team of the 20th century.

The hard lessons Rocky Bleier learned early in his life that helped him overcome adversity and reach his goals, have paid off after football. Some of those lessons are seen between the lines in the popular book on his life, *Fighting Back,* and an ABC-TV movie of the week by the same name.

In this book, Rocky shares experiences from his storied past that entertain, inspire and provide guidance to retirees and their families for reaching their financial, retirement and estate planning goals.

CONTENTS

INTRODUCTION

We live in a culture of opportunity, not necessarily a culture of entitlement. This is based on the simple premise that as long as we have choices, we are free. But with choice comes responsibility. The responsibility to ourselves is to be informed, to know what is taking place within our lives. Being informed and having the courage to act on that information are the responsibilities and opportunities afforded by freedom.

Basically, we have two choices in life. One is to be less than we're capable of being – to do less, have less impact, learn less, earn less money. Or we can choose to do more: Be more involved, more informed, more fulfilled, have more impact, make more of a difference in other people's lives.

Assuming that the vast majority of people set out to be the best that they can be, why is it that some people take action and succeed, when others elect to do nothing and fail? In the world of sports, why do some teams seem to win all the time, while others always seem to be perpetually losing? Financially, why are some people "set for life," while others struggle to get by? What ingredients enable us individually and collectively to reach the best results for ourselves and our families?

To answer that question, I'd like to tell you a story – my story. We all have a story of how we got to where we are today. The roads that we've taken may vary, but the lessons we've learned along the way are pretty much the same. We've all experienced ups and downs, successes and failures, opportunities and barriers. And here we are, still trying to do more and do it better.

Most of my life I have been involved in the world of sports – football, specifically. I still love the game, but it's not what I do anymore. No, I'm well past that point in life.

In fact, I'm 65, which for years has been the "golden number," the start of a well-deserved retirement after years of hard work. The beginning of a new phase of life when you can do the things you've been waiting for – a little travel maybe, or spending more time with family and friends, pursuing a life-long goal...and the list of retirement dreams goes on.

Then again, people today are leading much longer and healthier lives than in the past. A lot of us just aren't ready to stop working at age 65, 75 – even older! We have retirement dreams, too, but for now they're still on the back burner. Sadly, that's also the case for many people who have been planning and looking forward to retiring at age 65, but now find themselves unable to retire because of unforeseen financial worries and constraints.

In recent years I have met so many people whose hopes and dreams for retirement have been crushed. Life savings all but obliterated by stock market losses, defaulted pension plans, taxes and unanticipated health problems. Again, the list goes on, and it's not a pleasant one.

I'm writing this book because I think some of my experiences from winning in football can be applied just as aptly to winning in retirement. Basic things like teamwork, commitment, leadership, trust and vision.

Even though football has been my life, my focus and my passion, I've come to realize that I share this world with some people who couldn't care less about it (and some of them may be reading this book at this very moment)!

Whether or not you like the game, keep reading and you'll find some valuable analogies between achieving success on the gridiron and attaining financial stability and peace of mind in retirement. Along the way, you'll get to know more about the individuals and experiences that made my years in football so rewarding, as well as some new money lessons I've come to learn later in life.

Yes, I was very fortunate for those years I played with that team in Pittsburgh. So much so that today they now allow me to wear four fantastic rings from Super Bowls IX, X, XIII and XIV.

By the way, do you know how many Steelers fans it takes to change a light bulb? Five. One to change the light bulb, the other four to talk about how great the 70s were! That's 1974 against the Minnesota Vikings, 1975 and 1978 against the Dallas Cowboys, and 1979 against the then-LA Rams.

Every time I wear those rings I'm reminded of the successes we had, along with the failures. The depths we slogged through as well as the heights we achieved.

I hope you notice that the word "we" is prominent in all these recollections. It wasn't through the work of any one individual that we had that amazing run of success. No, we had a game plan, and we had an extraordinary team of people intensely focused on a single outcome, a shared vision.

It's no coincidence that that's also exactly what you need to have an amazing run of success in retirement.

TEAM MATTERS – For the first time in franchise history the Steelers went to the Super Bowl in 1974. (Yes, we won.) Like any successful team, we were individuals working toward a common purpose and goal: winning. A good retirement plan operates by the same fundamentals. The goal? A safe, worry-free retirement.

CHAPTER 1

YOUR GAME PLAN
AND YOUR TEAM

Throughout our lives we've heard many defini-
tions of the word "team." How about the acronym,
"Together Everyone Achieves More?" What about
"There's no 'I' in 'team'?" I'd like to share one more with
you, courtesy of my old coach, Chuck Noll, who said:
"A team is a group of individuals coming together for a
common purpose and a common goal. Along the way, each
individual has his own responsibility."

In football, the team's common purpose is to play the
game, and the team members' common goal is to win the
game. Responsibilities of the head coach and coaching staff
include getting the right players, putting them in the right
positions, supervising training, and ultimately arming
them with the best offensive and defensive game plans.
Players are responsible for following those game plans –
whether they like them or not – and executing them to the
best of their ability.

When I walked off the field and into the locker room,
I wanted to be able to look at myself in the mirror and

honestly say I did everything I possibly could to make that plan work. If each and every team member could do that, chances were very good that we, as a whole, accomplished a victory that day.

This single principle is one of the most important fundamentals in your retirement. Responsibility for yourself and responsibility for your loved ones are two powerful priorities held together by a common glue of trust and commitment.

In these uncertain times, making difficult financial decisions can be extremely uncomfortable. You have to be able to look your advisor in the eye and say, "I need to do this for me and my family" – no matter how formidable the goals might seem – and trust yourself and your advisor enough to know that, together, you can and will make it happen.

The first time my teammates and I had the opportunity to play in the Super Bowl (Super Bowl IX), was in 1974 against the Minnesota Vikings down in New Orleans at old Tulane Stadium. To put that game into perspective, the largest man in the Viking's defensive line weighed in at 265 pounds. The largest man on our offensive line, Jon Kolb, weighed in at 255 pounds. As a matter of fact, our starting offensive guards in that game weighed 217 and

NEW MONEY LESSON

Successful retirement plans are built on commitment:

• *Commitment to fulfilling our personal responsibilities and obligations*

• *Commitment to fulfilling our responsibilities to family and others we love and care about*

214 pounds, respectively, not even the size of a substantial high school football guard by today's standards!

The average salary in the NFL was $55,000 a year, and I was getting $25,000 a year. But you know what? I knew I was going to make more money in those playoff games than I made all year long. Pretty big incentive if you think about it. I like incentives. I like the idea that if I do my part and our team wins, I get rewarded for delivering.

Today, the average salary in the NFL is $1.3 million, and players make less than one-tenth of that in the playoff games they're in.

That's just one example of how incentives to succeed have diminished over the years. In the "new world" of

NEW MONEY LESSON

Time is not on our side.

No one is going to swoop in and save you and your family if you haven't formulated and executed a solid game plan for retirement.

Your team is not going to win the championship if you haven't drawn up a comprehensive plan that takes all contingencies into consideration, or if you simply haven't done what it takes to see it through to completion.

sweeping government bailouts, entitlement programs and staggering debt, the concept of responsibility has been seriously eroded. This sends the wrong signal to people who were brought up to know better...people like you and me.

Too many people today are paralyzed when it comes to retirement planning – overwhelmed by the economic roller coaster and not knowing where to turn for sound advice. It's understandable, but still unfortunate. It's just the way things are.

Yes, much is different today. Football players are bigger and they're faster. And because of that, strategies have changed both offensively and defensively. What hasn't changed, from the game's inception to this day, is that it's still about fundamentals. Blocking and tackling, running and throwing, about having a game plan and executing that game plan. It's about hard work, dedication and commitment. It's about having a passion, leadership, a team and a vision.

It's still about individuals coming together for a common purpose and a common goal – and those fundamentals not only apply to football, but also are crucial to safely planning your future.

I've always understood the fundamentals of football. How to improve the game became obvious to me shortly after I left Notre Dame and came to Pittsburgh. Specifically: Better players + better coaching = better results.

Unfortunately, I didn't always understand the fundamentals of a safe retirement. That is, until I met an extraordinary young man who is now my business partner, Matt Zagula.

I met Matt through his work with veterans – a very important group of people to me. He had developed an extremely powerful financial and benefits training program specifically for our country's service men and women.

Matt had earned a stellar reputation because of the help he had provided many veterans in sorting out their financial troubles, but still I approached him with some skepticism. His work at the Veterans Benefit Institute checked out, though, as did his later work with retirees at the Estate and Elder Planning Center. Advisors from across the country sought out Matt's counsel – advisors appearing on CNBC, MSNBC TV and in *The Wall Street Journal* and *Forbes*.

I was initially curious and unsure, but over time Matt's motivation to help others became inarguably clear. It is for that reason that today Matt and I are good friends and partners at Bleier Zagula, where we specialize in financial planning specifically geared toward creating retirement income for retirees who need income right now, and the soon to be retired, who will need income in the future.

You might think I'm an unlikely "financial guy," but you've got to agree that at 65 years old, I'm smack-dab in the middle of the retirement age demographic. And guess what? Retired professional football player or not, I'm dealing with many of the same dilemmas facing thousands of other 65-year-olds across the country. (Remember, I didn't make the big bucks these kids are making today!)

Here's a little insight into my personal retirement situation. I might be approaching retirement years, but I have a wife and four children, two of whom are young, and seven grandchildren. I'm not just preparing for retirement: I have two college educations to plan for, plus the need for dependable income to last throughout my lifetime as well as my wife's. Like many of you reading this book, I realize that I can't wait five or 10 years for the market to bounce back or interest rates to go up. I have to take action immediately.

In a way, it reminds me of what happened when free agency came to football. Let me explain. Free agency has turned out to be one of the pivotal developments in the game. That reality hit home to me about four years after its inception, when two expansion teams, the Jacksonville Jaguars and the Carolina Panthers, found themselves in the championship games of their respective divisions after being in existence for only 18 months. It was at that moment in time that the perceptions and expectations of owners and fans immediately went into overdrive.

Before that, the model for building a team was five years – five years for a new head coach to come on board, assemble the players, turn a franchise around and get a team into championship mode. Now, all of a sudden, two upstarts had come in and done it in just 18 short months!

THE HOME TEAM – *Top photo:* My daughter Samantha and son Adri, now grown with children of their own. *Bottom photo:* My daughters Elly and Rosie, and my wife Jan.

The owners wanted to know – and rightfully so – if *they* can do it in 18 months, why can't *my team* do it in the next 18 months?

As it turned out, 18 months to turn out a championship team didn't replace the traditional five-year model. Today the expectation is more like two to three years – not as extreme as 18 months, but a significant change in expectations, nonetheless.

Did we like it? Was it fair? It didn't matter. It was and is reality. Ditto the new retirement landscape.

I t used to be that people stayed at their jobs for many years and retired with full pensions and Social Security benefits. They painstakingly built their nest eggs to serve as backup funds to dip into when expenses surpassed the guaranteed retirement income of their company pensions and their government-issued Social Security checks. It was a reliable formula for a comfortable, secure retirement.

Somewhere along the way, most companies replaced their pension programs with 401(k)s. Rather than guaranteed pension amounts, many people's retirement savings are now subject to the swings of the stock market and interest rate fluctuations. If your time to retire happens to hit when the market is way down, the mathematics of loss can be devastatingly harsh and your retirement security compromised. You no longer have 20 or 30 working years left to build your savings back up.

Do we like it? Is it fair? Again, it doesn't matter. It was and is reality.

That's why I decided this was the right business for me. I want to help retirees and those approaching retirement come up with a solid game plan to achieve their retirement goals in today's "Rocky" environment (excuse the pun). I want to share some of the new money lessons I've learned over the past few years.

There might not be an official Super Bowl in this line of work, but seeing retirees and fellow baby boomers get the ball (their hard-earned savings) safely to their end zone (reaching their goals in their retirement years) certainly is as rewarding as winning a championship.

THE BLEIER ZAGULA TEAM – *Top photo:* (standing) Aaron Gurskey, Matt Zagula, attorney Pam Zagula, Rocky Bleier, Pam Weaver, Denise Beatty, Debbie Shay; (seated) Leah Pettengill, Bonnie Zagula, Alicia Licause, Carol Feeney. *Bottom photo:* Our Pittsburgh office at 969 Greentree Road.

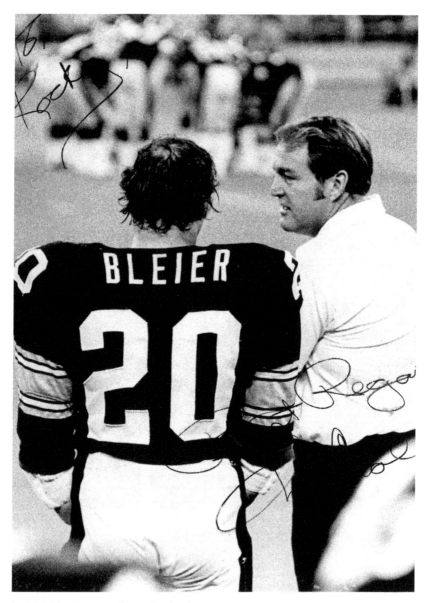

LEADERSHIP – Head coach Chuck Noll built an unforgettable championship dynasty that I was privileged to be a part of. Like any great leader, he had the innate ability to gather the right individuals and skillfully manage their interaction.

CHAPTER 2

VISION + LEADERSHIP = SUSTAINABLE SUCCESS

Consider football's great dynasties: the Green Bay Packers of the 1960s, the Steelers of the 1970s, the 49ers of the 1980s, the Cowboys of the 1990s, or the Buffalo Bills, the only team to go to four straight Super Bowls. What's the key to their enduring success?

They all had great coaches and talented players – that's a given. If I could single out one element that set them apart from their competitors, though, it's that each team shared a defined, collectively bought-into, long-term goal. A vision, not for one season or two, but a comprehensive plan for what they would achieve, year after year.

If you're like me, your long-term financial vision is something like this:

- To have the income you need to live comfortably in retirement
- To ensure that your surviving spouse has ample income after your death
- To leave a financial legacy for your family, if financially possible

How do you deliver that sustainable success? At times it helps to look back into our past and our culture. In this case, I have to take you back to 1933, when Arthur J. Rooney spent $2,500 to buy a franchise in the National Football League. He brought the franchise back to Pittsburgh, and he moved a northside sandlot football team into the fledgling NFL.

For the next 40 years, that team had a destiny... to lose! It operated on short-term gains, week-to-week, month-to-month, year-to-year, passing the hat. Every now and then they'd bring in a marquee player to sell some tickets. Even so, Pittsburgh was the doormat of the league. It was always the same old Steelers refrain: "Wait until next year, maybe something will change."

The team took on the aura of its culture. Think about Pittsburgh, about western Pennsylvania at that time. Think about the immigrants who settled in the area, working the coal mines and steel mills, moving the barges up and down the river. Tough, hard-nosed, blue-collar workers, putting in 12- and 14-hour days just to keep a roof over their heads, a meal on the table.

A rough group, just like the team. You played the Steelers, let me tell you, they'd beat the crap out of you. They'd never win, but they could knock you around pretty good.

Yet it changed. Not right away, but when the owners, the Rooneys, went outside the organization and brought in a guy by the name of Chuck Noll. What he brought to the Steelers was leadership, and he instilled the will and an expectation to win. Noll had a Pygmalion effect, helping his players reach their full potential and even expand it.

Leaders are committed to building great game plans, and they take responsibility for the outcomes. A large part of my motivation to start Bleier Zagula was that I found those leadership traits missing in the western Pennsylvania advisory marketplace.

You see, in the world of leadership, the ability to lead is conferred by those who need or desire guidance from a trusted source. We players, for example, gave Noll the power to lead, not by entitlement, but because we wanted to be better. We believed we could do better, and so did he.

Here's how all this pertains to you. If you believe that you can have a successful, sustainable retirement plan, what I will do for you is share my beliefs about the importance of financial safety and working with the right team. (That's right, you have a choice! Football players get drafted, but you get to choose who you want on your retirement planning team.) My team and I can guide you in the direction that I believe will lead you to greater success in achieving your retirement goals.

Let me share with you another important lesson I learned, not from football, but from my army days. I was in the service with a grizzly old drill sergeant who loved to engage in little one-on-one chats, nose to nose, whenever he had the opportunity. One day, before I could escape his formidable presence, he spun me around, pinned me against a wall, and jabbed a burly finger in my chest.

"Bleier, I'm going to tell you this, and I'm only going to tell you this once. When you're put in charge of a platoon squad, by God, you take charge. And when you're in charge, have the courage to do what's right. Not what somebody else thinks is right, not necessarily what even your superior thinks is right, but what *you* think is right. What's right for the situation, right for the detail, and more importantly, what's right for the men."

Today, I can so easily swap the words "for the men" with "for your family." It certainly takes courage to take charge of your financial future (and theirs).

Another lesson I took away from that little "chat" with the drill sergeant was about courage.

Obviously, courage means not being a coward or shirking responsibility. We know that, right? But it's not necessarily about the big Hollywood, ending either. One choice might make for a better scene in a movie – guns blazing, the hero deciding on a hunch to "take the hill," or whatever. But that's not always how real-life courage plays out.

NEW MONEY LESSON

If there's only one thing that you get out of this book, make it this:

• *Get up and start taking a serious look at your retirement options.*

I view courage as applying what we know – repeat, KNOW – to move forward, to take action. And, by God, we need to do that every day of our lives.

The decision to do nothing is, in fact, a decision. Failure to act is an act of complacency, an act of blind acceptance. With the economics of loss so harsh, a failure to act is most certainly not advisable. If there's only one thing that you get out of this book, make it this: Get up and start taking a serious look at your retirement options.

Now back to Chuck Noll and the first real meeting we had with him as our new head coach. He stood before us, not with the demeanor of a drill sergeant, but more like a straight-shooting businessman explaining a major change in company strategy. He said: "Gentleman, I've watched every film of every practice you've had and every game you've played over the last three years. I can tell why you're losing. You're just not any good.

"By the time this training camp is over, most of you won't be here. Not that you won't want to be here, or that you're not good people... I don't mean that. No, the problem is that you haven't made a commitment to raise standards, a commitment to excellence. Some of you might not have the talent to perform at that level. Where that's the case, I'm going to have to go out and find some people who do."

Think about Noll's words – harsh, yes, but true. So many retirees and pre-retirees accept sub-optimal results, poor service and incomplete planning, but they don't want to offend their advisors by telling them so. All the while, they're losing yardage, getting pushed back to their side of the field. What do you do when it's fourth and long? You don't want to be answering that question when the decision affects the rest of your life!

I respect Chuck Noll for telling us the truth, making us accountable and demanding more. He just kept upping the bar, not only within the existing team, but also through the players he brought in.

For example, in the 1969 draft he went out and got a guy by the name of Joe Greene from North Texas State. The next year he found a pretty good quarterback in Louisiana by the name of Terry Bradshaw. That same year he found Mel Blount, a cornerback from Southern University.

NEW MONEY LESSON

The right coach is critical.

How do you win against what may seem like insurmountable challenges of retirement planning? Find an advisor who knows how to build a retirement plan that prevents loss, even in today's challenging economic environment.

In 1971 he went up to Penn State and got a linebacker, Jack Ham. The next year at the same school he nabbed Ham's former teammate, running back Franco Harris. In 1974 he got two receivers, Lynn Swann and John Stallworth; a middle linebacker out of Kent State named Jack Lambert; and a center out of Wisconsin, Mike Webster.

And that's just a few of Noll's picks – a few of the ones in the National Football League Hall of Fame, that is. They raised the standard for all of us and made us better teammates, better people and better leaders.

Football, like money, is about building a solid foundation. Over time you add the right refinements to enhance the core, ultimately combining the best assets into a sustainable and comprehensive long-term plan designed for success.

BASIC GAME PLAN, FLAWLESS EXECUTION – Legendary quarterback Terry Bradshaw (right) called his own plays. Four simple plays that earned us four Super Bowl championships. Retirement income planning isn't so different: It's simple as long as your team follows the game plan and executes it flawlessly.

CHAPTER 3

SIMPLE WINS

Some people underestimated our illustrious quarterback, Terry Bradshaw. Here he was, the number one pick of the NFL all those years ago, a big man – 6'3", 225 pounds – an all-American blond, blue-eyed matinee idol who could launch a football 80 yards with a flick of his wrist.

Terry had been a quarterback virtually all of his life, from junior high on, but he'd never called his own plays. Early on, coach Noll took him aside and said, "I'll teach you how to read defenses; I'll show you what plays to call. But you have to make the decision that you want to become a great quarterback. And when you do, young man, you will take charge of this team." And the rest is history.

If there's one aspect of Bradshaw's career that he's proudest of, it's that he called his own plays. If you ever visit the Football Hall of Fame, you'll see Terry's bust with a biography underneath. One line will jump right out at you, for it boldly states, "And I called my own plays."

That simple fact has been reinforced not only in his mind, but also in the mind of the public, from the day he retired to this past football season. On any given Sunday, the host of the broadcast panel on Fox Sports will bring up the topic of the young quarterbacks today and how difficult it is for them because of the size and speed of the players and the complexities of the defense.

Howie Long will jump in with a very erudite response, and Jimmy Johnson will inject the coach's perspective. But what they actually need is someone who has been in the quarterback's shoes. As the camera pans across the panel, Bradshaw comes into view, along with a little gleam shooting off his forehead. I can recite his response along with him, virtually word for word, as he says, "Oh, you guys are right. I mean, I don't know how those young quarter-backs today do it. Those guys are huge, they're big, they're strong, they're fast, and defenses are more complex than I ever saw in the past..."

Then you wait for it...Here it comes...

"But I will tell you one thing," he'll continue. "These quarterbacks today don't call their own plays. Call me an old guy, call me a dinosaur, I don't care. At least I called my own plays. Roger Staubach, as smart as that man is, did not call his own plays. I called my own plays." And he'll go on like that as long as they'll let him.

What he DOESN'T tell you is that we only had four plays! Two running plays and two passing plays. Period. But you know what? Terry did a wonderful job. He called

---

NEW MONEY LESSON

Keep it simple.

If you execute with great care and precision, your retirement plan needn't be complex.

---

those four plays and earned us four Super Bowl championships. Simple, straightforward, well-executed games.

R etirement income planning is just like Terry's four plays: It can be simple as long as your team executes it properly and follows the game plan. Here is the simple game plan that I learned from Matt Zagula.

There are three basic "buckets" of money you need during your retirement years:

---

1. **"Now" money** – The monthly amount you need (in addition to your Social Security and pension benefits) to maintain your current lifestyle for the next two to six years.

2. **Growth money** – Funds to park safely in interest-earning investment vehicles (e.g., fixed annuities,

CDs, insured deposits, government bonds). A skilled retirement income specialist can work out how much to invest – and for how long – in several accounts so you'll have secure income for the rest of your life. Advisors who know the right plays will take all contingencies into consideration, including:

- "In case" money to cover **long-term health-care** if the need arises (as it does for 50% of Americans over 65 years of age)

- **Inflation,** which year-over-year will continue to increase the prices of food, gasoline, heating oil and other necessities

- The **death of a spouse,** which can dramatically reduce the surviving partner's Social Security and/or pension payments

- Structuring investments to keep **taxes** as low as possible

3. **Legacy money** – Money to leave your heirs. Again, a skilled retirement income specialist can help you structure these accounts to best meet your particular goals.

And there you have it. A simple game plan based on plain old math: Money you need sooner is tucked into no-risk accounts; while money you won't need to access for a few years is secured in low-risk accounts with possibly higher returns to grow for the future.

Leaving little subjected to the whims of Wall Street, everything's in a safe place until needed.

Basic, yes. But when executed flawlessly it's a plan that can yield a well-deserved championship: a secure future with lifetime income and a lasting legacy for your children.

MY FIRST RETIREMENT – After my last game with the Steelers I enjoyed a "mini retirement" of sorts, but it was years before I started thinking about retirement in the true sense of the word. A bit of advice: Don't wait too long.

TRUST – The offensive line that I trusted to open the holes that allowed me to have a 1,000-yard rushing season in 1976. From left, Ray Pinney, Gerry "Moose" Mullin, me, Ray Mansfield, Jon Kolb, Mike Webster, coach Dan Radakovich.

CHAPTER 4

CREATING A CULTURE OF TRUST

I believe one of the key things that changed under Terry Bradshaw's leadership was the culture of the team. As you surely know, football has its own inimitable culture. It's the only time of the year when we as mature adults can be adolescents once again. We yell, we scream, we wear our team's colors. Heck, some of us paint our faces, put numbers on our bodies and have beer cans growing out the sides of our heads – a true Pittsburgh original. All of these are part of the culture of football.

And within the culture of the game there are subcultures. Think about it. There's an offensive culture, which is completely different than a defensive culture. One of the things you learn in an offensive culture, from the day you put the pads on to the day you take them off, is that only one person speaks in the offense: the quarterback. The rest of you remain silent. You're just supposed to think about your responsibility, not confuse the issue, think about the snap count. That reality is reinforced week after week, month after month, year after year, level after level. The quarterback speaks and the rest of you keep quiet.

NEW MONEY LESSON

It's your responsibility.

• *Be an informed and open-minded manager of your own money.*

• *Take decisive action toward planning ideas that you understand and feel comfortable with.*

So, you have a young quarterback coming out of college into his first year in the NFL. What does he believe? He believes he has to lead. Whether or not he's prepared, he needs to take charge. Terry Bradshaw felt the same way. At least at first.

All of that began to change in 1974, toward the end of the season. We were winning some games. We had momentum, which is very important going into the end of the season. This particular game was crucial. It was the fourth quarter and we had a slight lead. It boiled down to a third and short situation – third and short! We needed to pick up a first down to control the ball, to potentially win the game.

Bradshaw had engaged in a heated dialogue with one of the defenders in the previous play. In the meantime, the official had picked up the ball, set it down and started the play clock. So by the time Terry got back into the huddle, the clock was ticking down. He had to decide which one of the four plays he needed to call. To complicate matters, we had four different formations in which we could run. So, by simple mathematics, there were 16 different combinations. With the play clock ticking down, Terry was sweating profusely from the forehead, and when he started to stammer I knew we were in trouble.

At the moment of no return, he needed to make the play or we were going to take a penalty and be forced out of position to make that first down. He looked up at his offensive line and said, "Hey, what do you guys want to run?"

I have to tell you in all honesty, ladies and gentlemen, I was somewhat shocked. Why? Because I was standing right next to him, me a Notre Dame grad, pretty smart guy (I think, anyway). He could have said, "Hey, Rocky, I need a little help, what do you think?" Did he do that? No. Franco was standing to his other side. Penn State grad, another smart guy. Did he say, "Hey, Franco, got any suggestions?" No.

Without thinking, Terry Bradshaw's first reaction was to turn to his offensive line. Not to take anything away from offensive linemen, but you have to understand, they get hit on every play. How bright can you be to put yourself in that position? And at a crucial moment Terry is asking them what they want to run!

NEW MONEY LESSON

Winning strategies are built on commitment.

Winning retirement plans are the result of mutual trust between advisors and clients – trust that's earned through actions and results demonstrating that the advisor is doing what's right for the client and the client is committed to the investment strategy.

Yet an amazing transformation took hold. They all stood up at once, and it was like years of repression fell from their shoulders. Their eyes got big, their jaws dropped open, their tongues loosened, and what spewed forth were things I had never heard before. "We can do this, we can block over here; Terry, just ram it right down the middle and we'll pick up the first down..."

And, bam, we got the first down, just like they said. They delivered.

It was not the last time Terry Bradshaw would go to the well when he got into trouble. But at that moment, the offensive line became part of a solution rather than mere participants in the game. They trusted Bradshaw, and he trusted them. There was buy-in. They were part of a team, part of working together.

That same kind of partnership forms when clients "bare" their financial selves to a financial planner, and the planner analyzes each individual's situation in detail to formulate the specific winning strategy for that client. The client knows the advisor fully understands his retirement needs and objectives, so he buys into the solution and together they implement it.

DETERMINED TO WIN – You win football games by crossing the goal line. You win in retirement by being committed to getting there.

WHO KNEW? – Franco Harris about to score one of the most unlikely touch-downs in football history. His remarkable scoop of the ball before it hit the ground embodied the concept of taking things into your own hands to keep from losing.

CHAPTER 5

IT DOESN'T TAKE AN IMMACULATE RECEPTION TO SCORE A RETIREMENT WIN

In 1972 for the first time in franchise history, the Steelers won the division championship. And it was during the playoffs that the team made one of the all-time great comebacks in football history. It all hinged on one play, which to Steelers fans and football aficionados became known as the Immaculate Reception. If I may, I would like to take you back to the last minute of that game.

It had been a toughly fought battle, and we had the lead, 6-0, on two field goals. But late in the game we allowed the Oakland Raiders to move the ball down to our 30-yard line. It was a third and long situation when Kenny Stabler, their quarterback, took the snap and dropped back. He looked downfield, hoping to get a first down, to keep the ball in play and maybe get his team in position to score.

We weren't going to let that happen, obviously. We had everyone covered – double-teamed where necessary. The only person uncovered was Stabler himself, who according to the reports wasn't much of a threat. He was a runner, not a scrambler. More of a loper, actually. As he dropped back and searched downfield, the middle of our defense opened up and Stabler had the audacity to tuck the ball under his arm and lope right through our defense.

The fans in the stands started screaming for the defense to respond. But by the time they did, Stabler was down to the five-yard line. Before anyone could get there, he dove to score and tied the game. Then they kicked for the extra point and took the lead.

Stunned silence as the fans recognized their same old Steelers. "Can't win the big game. We had it, but let it slip right through our fingers. Maybe next year'll be different."

But it wasn't quite over. On the ensuing kickoff we got the ball back on our 30-yard line. Three incomplete passes by our illustrious quarterback, Mr. Bradshaw, left us with a fourth down and 70 situation to score and win this game. No timeouts. Thirty-two seconds left on the clock.

Bradshaw took the snap, dropped back and looked downfield for an open receiver. An instant later, the left side of our line broke and the right side of their defensive line poured through, putting even more pressure on Terry. Right before he was hit, he looked downfield and saw Frenchy Fuqua, running back, oh, about 30 yards. As Terry was going down, he released the ball, and being the great athlete that he is, the ball came off like a shot – hard, fast and furious. And Frenchy was downfield waiting for it.

Jack Tatum, the defensive back for the Oakland Raiders, was coached as all defensive backs are coached, that when the ball is thrown you get there, smack it down, intercept it, or at least make the tackle so the other team can't advance the ball. So Tatum was on his high horse, Frenchy was waiting, and the ball was coming.

It was Tatum, Frenchy and the ball, and the inevitable happened: All three arrived at the same point at the same time, and the ball caromed into the air and back down, on its way to hit the turf and end the game for a Raiders win.

When out of the backfield, the rookie sensation from Penn State, Franco Harris, scooped the ball off his shoestrings, and before anyone could react, he crossed the 50, 45, 35, 25, 15, sailed through the end zone and scored!

The place exploded with 58,000 fans yelling, screaming and stomping their feet. The team rushed down the sideline to congratulate Franco, and when we got to the end zone, there he was, just standing all by himself. So we did what everyone has done from the beginning of time, given those circumstances. We jumped on top of him, and more piled on top of us.

Yet there was no indication of whether or not Franco had actually scored a touchdown, because the officials hadn't seen exactly what happened. Did the ball hit Tatum or Frenchy? Did the ball hit the ground? The rule at the time was that the ball had to hit a defender before an offensive player could catch it.

The referees huddled on the field. "What happened?" "I don't know." "Did the ball hit the ground?" "I don't know." "Did it hit Tatum, did it hit Frenchy?" "I don't know." "Well, what *do* you know?" "It wasn't my responsibility." "I was on the other side of the field." "My back was turned." "My eyes were closed." "Hey, don't look at me!"

It was like any other business meeting when things aren't going particularly well and management is going to be called in. Referee Fred Swearingen took it upon himself to go to the sidelines and look for a phone, which eventually was located in the old Pirates dugout (the Steelers' original name). He called up to the press box and got Art McNally on the other end. Art was the supervisor in charge of the officials, and when he heard Fred, the first thing he said was, "Fred, is that you?" "Yes, it is." "Well, you're not supposed to be talking to me."

"I understand that, but this is a pretty big game," Fred said. "Did you see what happened? Can you give us any help, any direction? Did the ball hit the ground, did he catch it, did it hit Tatum, did it hit Frenchy, did it do anything?"

ART: Fred, where are you calling me from?

FRED: I'm on the sidelines in the Pirates dugout.

ART: What's going on down there?

FRED: What's going on down here? Can't you see there's bedlam going on down here! I have 200, 300, 400 people pouring out of the stands right in front of me. And let me tell you this, Art, there's not a whole lot of security down here.

ART: Fred, I want you to think about this for a moment. What stadium are you in?

With that, Fred hung up the phone, walked over to the goal line and raised his arms. And that's how we won the game. It was like the football gods finally changed their minds, and we finally won a big game. And for us there was hope in the air.

Today when I think of the Immaculate Reception and compare it to my retirement, I can immediately relate that game to the current economic situations we face. Both then and now, the message is a powerful statement of not blindly accepting loss.

You see, if Franco had let the ball hit the ground, like many players would have, the game was all but lost. I believe that extraordinary catch speaks to us in two different, yet connected, ways:

First, an unwillingness to accept loss. As we get older, our tolerance for risk should go down since the economics of loss are so harsh. On the facing page is an eye-opening visual that was shared with me, that I would now like to share with you. It's a simple exercise explaining how much money you need to gain after a loss just to get back to your original principal. The big question for us approaching retirement – and certainly a huge question for those in retirement – is, do we have enough time left to get it back?

A very interesting recent study by the Putnam Institute teaches us that if we put more than 25% of our money into the stock market, we are subjecting ourselves to a potential income loss that may significantly affect our retirement lifestyle. And the really interesting thing is that this institute is funded by Putnam Investments, which sells mutual funds! So, assessing risk and having an unwillingness to accept loss while headed into your retirement is a significant factor to building a solid fiscal foundation.

Next, this memorable event in football history illustrates the value of having the courage to act. I know that today, in these potentially uncertain and

NEW MONEY LESSON

There's no time for risk.

If you invested $100,000 into a mutual fund that experienced a 20% loss, you would lose $20,000. The account value on your next statement would be $80,000.

Question: *For you to get your statement balance back to $100,000, will a 20% gain recoup your loss?*

> *Let's crunch the numbers:*
> *$80,000 x 20% = $16,000*
>
> *$80,000 (beginning balance)*
> *+ 16,000*
> ———————
> *$96,000*

Answer: *No, a 20% loss followed by a 20% gain does not get you your principal back. In fact, to regain your original principal balance you will need to get a 25% return.*

unstable economic times, we are encouraged to hunker down and plan for the long haul, to believe that the losses we see on our statements are not "real" until we sell. You know the expressions, "It's just paper losses, no matter how real they feel to you," or "It'll come back, just hold on."

As I sit here and write this as a healthy man 65 years young, I'm not sure that advice makes sense. I plan on continuing to work as long as I can – I enjoy it. But I can't control genetic factors that may influence my health, just as I can't control the economy. I hope that my good health continues, and I hope our elected officials act in our best interests and don't extend debts and spending misbehaviors that ultimately my children and grandchildren will be burdened with in the future.

I frequently teach the value of hope and belief. But one cannot realistically be certain of the eventual outcome when it comes to this economic situation, the future of healthcare costs and how retirement income can be safely created and relied on for a lifetime after our working years end.

The courage I am speaking of now is the confidence to rely upon yourself to manage your finances in a way that is logical to you. Perhaps one of the most significant moments in my relationship with my business partner, Matt Zagula, was when I asked him who he believes people should trust when dealing with their own money and retirement planning issues. I, of course, expected him to say, "They should trust me, Rocky." But this was no joke. He was very serious as he explained a core belief of his – a belief that I now share. He said, "Rocky, the person you should trust the most with your finances is yourself. And that goes for everybody."

The explanation of that surprising response was simply that more people lose money in investments and planning ideas due to lack of understanding and over-complexity. Matt and I firmly believe in simple plans that make sense in very basic, easy to understand terms.

O ur "math over markets" approach may seem overly simplistic at first, especially to those accustomed to the guesswork and expectations – often unfulfilled – of market investing.

It takes courage to be open to a different approach to retirement and how retirement income can be generated on a contractually certain basis.

Financial marketing leads us to believe that the Wall Street-created investment vehicles, such as mutual funds, are our surest path to financial prosperity. This is simply not true. Many academic studies suggest quite a different outcome. Quite frankly, some of my own past investments that sounded almost too good to be true certainly were just that. My guess is that my experience with investments is not that different from yours.

NEW MONEY LESSON

Do the math!

Retirement plans that are validated by math – good old addition, subtraction and multiplication – are the most logical choice for the vast majority of retirees, not scenarios that are dependent on market events, which are unpredictable at best.

The Immaculate Reception had a lot to do with "path dependency," which means that each player acted out his assigned role. Frenchy did his part by "playing the ball," and thankfully he didn't catch it but instead tipped it into the air allowing Franco to scoop that pass from Bradshaw just inches from the ground. Tatum, the defensive back, did his part by "playing the man," but that gave Franco the opportunity to catch the ball and run for that historic touchdown.

The game of football is based on systems and on accepted principals, but sometimes unexpected situations arise, and the systems – although executed according to plan – result in a much different outcome. In the world of money, like football, it's all about fractional seconds, your position and your willingness to make positive changes to effectuate a successful outcome.

Let's look at another revealing study shared with me by my friend Matt. This example (from the Wharton Financial Institutions Center) is based on rates of return for different periods and overall five-year performance. We can use the performance of the Standard & Poor's 500 Index (S&P 500) to illustrate:

1997-2002
9.39%

But start investing just one year later and the five-year performance is quite different:

1998-2003
-0.42%

Oh, what a difference a year can make!

Now let's see the huge performance differential year to year by looking at the index, starting again just one year apart:

2002-2007
13.37%

One year later and the performance draws down over 10% per year:

2003-2008
3.18%

So, if Franco takes half a step in the wrong direction prior to breaking on that tipped pass, the Immaculate Reception becomes just another missed pass, just another statistic of failure, and we lose that game.

There are many powerful money lessons to be learned by this historic play, but the most meaningful to me is simply taking the responsibility to be an informed and open-minded manager of your own money, and then taking decisive action toward planning ideas that you understand and feel comfortable with. I can speak from my own experience that this simple concept is simply underutilized.

UNEXPECTED – Thousands of fans rushed the field following the Immaculate Reception, and it had to be cleared so the point-after conversion could be kicked. The final score was Pittsburgh 13, Oakland 7.

PATH DEPENDENCE – In our 1976 season both Franco Harris (right) and I rushed for over 1,000 yards, an opportunity created by exceptional execution on the part of our offensive line. Here we're pictured with coach Dick Hoak (center).

CHANGE OF UNIFORM – After my rookie year with the Steelers I was drafted by the U.S. Army. I shipped out in May 1969 and served in the Americal Division. In combat, risk is constant and not always manageable. Today I'm glad to be in the business of minimizing risk and helping people achieve peace of mind in their retirement years.

CHAPTER 6

NO ONE WAKES UP EXPECTING TO GET SHOT (EVEN IN THE JUNGLES OF VIETNAM)

UN-expected, UN-welcome, UN-prepared and UN-certain. Just a few of the UNs we face when something happens that we really didn't ever want to deal with. I can assure you that I did not wake up one morning expecting to follow our point man into a nasty firefight that led to four members of our squad losing their lives and many, including me, being seriously injured.

I've participated in team sports for as long as I can remember. For those of you who have served in the armed forces, you understand that the military is like a team. There are squads and sister squads, and the efforts of the team are coordinated by the senior officers who position the troops in the right place at the right time to meet certain objectives. There is a lot in common with team sports, but with much graver consequences when mistakes are made.

There were definitely mistakes made the day I was both shot and injured by a grenade. A breakdown in communication triggered a sequence of events leading to a less than desirable outcome. Some of the errors could have been avoided, but others were probably inevitable, outside the control of our squad, the point man or the senior officer.

I'd like to examine both scenarios: how to avoid common errors and how to handle bad circumstances beyond our control.

It makes perfect sense that we would all seek to avoid costly errors. We take in relevant information, and based on that information we make the best decisions we can. This was true for me that day in Vietnam, and it's true for most of us each and every day. We make choices, sometimes good and sometimes not so good. These decisions set into motion a sequence of events that can move us either toward a positive or negative outcome – or sometimes both.

Not so long ago I read a financial article about the problems facing the Social Security system. Based on data current at that time, the article cited that the system would fail in 2036 due to underfunding. A few short months later, I read that the government needed to increase its amount of allowable debt just to meet the *next month's* Social Security obligations. Somehow a problem that was meant to strike some 24 years into the future became relevant, real and downright scary in just a few months.

NEW MONEY LESSON

Rely on logic, not luck.

As the economic situation in this country continues to unravel, the decisions you make based on logic and self-reliance are far more likely to propel you in a positive direction than those based on hopeful thinking or what "used to be."

Recently my business partner, Matt, and I watched an old *60 Minutes* clip featuring David Walker, the U.S. comptroller general from 1998 to 2008. In the clip, titled "Wake-Up Call," Mr. Walker explained that the numbers our country faces with the Social Security and Medicare systems are disastrous – and this aired in 2007! Walker eventually resigned in frustration over Congress' lack of immediate action to these issues.

Meanwhile, here we are well on our way to 2012, and those same problems just keep compounding. Plus, there's the added burden of multiple bailouts – AIG, Fannie Mae, Freddie Mac and a number of other financial services and banking firms. Not to mention the decline in housing and real estate prices and, most recently, Standard & Poor's downgrade of the nation's credit rating.

Whatever happened to accountability and rational thinking? Believe it or not, they still exist if you know where to look. (And never forget, if you're having trouble finding them elsewhere, just look in the mirror.)

Our firm, Bleier Zagula, was built on four key principles that we believe are essential to success in this new era of self-reliance. They are:

- **Safety first!**
- **Reasonable rates of return**
- **Simplicity**
- **Retirement income** that is guaranteed to be there for life... yours and your spouse's (if you are married)

Think about it: Health costs are going up, government programs are being reduced or eliminated, and with the mounting financial obligations of our country, taxes must rise. What does this mean to our generation? We need reliable income throughout our retirement years.

Do I wish I could rely on Social Security and Medicare to provide the benefits I need and have been counting on? Of course. Do I wish our squad could have avoided firefight that day in Vietnam? Absolutely I do. The errors made that day cost lives. Given the present perils of the economy, errors made today may not put lives at immediate risk, but do create enormous risk of financial loss. Be smart and follow your own best judgment.

Then there are unseen and therefore uncontrollable risk factors, such as serious health problems leading to long-term disability. Just like I didn't expect to wake up in a hospital with shrapnel in my leg, many like me don't expect to face a debilitating stroke or heart attack, or a diagnosis of Alzheimer's, ALS or Parkinson's disease.

Unexpected, perhaps. But we have to consider the statistics from AARP, Met Life and GE Financial (now Genworth) informing us that one in two Americans over

---

NEW MONEY LESSON

Know what you can prepare for.

As part of a comprehensive retirement plan, one must consider all of the following:

* *Lifetime retirement income*

* *Asset protection from long-term care expense*

* *Avoidance of excessive taxation*

* *The financial planning impact of legal estate planning documents*

NEW MONEY LESSON

One of two people over age 65 will need long-term care.

Whether it's at-home care, an assisted living facility or a nursing home, the expense of long-term medical assistance can make a health crisis a financial crisis as well. Do yourself a favor and factor this very real possibility into your retirement income plan.

---

the age of 65 will at some point require skilled assistance to conduct the basic activities of daily life. This dreaded possibility and the financial consequences are risks that just cannot be ignored.

Early on when I read my partner Matt Zagula's first book, *Invasion of the Money Snatchers, a Practical Guide to Protecting Your $tuff from Creditors, Predators and a Government Gone Wild,* I realized how much I did NOT know about long-term care and planning for a disability. Imagine a situation that arises 50% of the time for people my age and up, and I knew virtually nothing about the subject at all!

If I thought there was a 50% chance my home was going to be robbed this evening and my family's well-being was in jeopardy, I can assure you I would take many precautions to protect them. That said, I was shocked to find that only 6% of retirees and those soon to be retired have purchased long-term care insurance. And, from Matt's book, I learned there are a number of options superior to traditional long-term care coverage to safeguard retirees from the same financial exposure.

Ideally, great planning has an UN-doing effect. You UN-do your lack of preparedness for the things in your future that can be controlled, and you have a charted-out course of action for the risk factors beyond your control.

LITTLE DID I KNOW – In a rare relaxed moment in Vietnam I had no idea that in a matter of weeks I'd be in a Tokyo hospital being told I wouldn't play football again. I didn't plan on being injured, but that didn't stop it from happening. Planning for long-term disability as we age isn't easy, but it's too costly a risk factor to ignore.

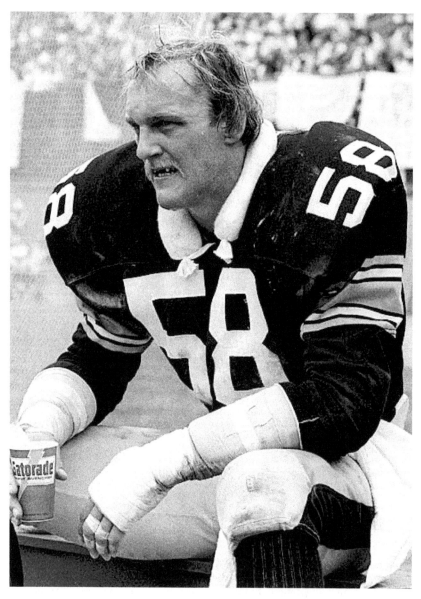

DEFENSE PERSONIFIED – Perhaps the greatest linebacker of all time, Jack Lambert proved that a good defense prevents losing. Jack hated to lose. Have you put a Lambert into your retirement plan?

CHAPTER 7

INVEST LIKE A LINEBACKER; ELIMINATE LOSS FROM THE EQUATION

The Steelers have a doctrine that must be honored by all team members and coaches alike. And that is, simply: *The other team can't win if they don't score.* Remember the "steel curtain" – the nickname given to the Steelers defensive line in the 1970s? The names in the lineup changed over the years, but the resilience of the steel curtain didn't. This is in no small part due to a great coach, Dick LeBeau, whose unique strategies capitalized on each individual's strengths within one amazing defensive unit.

Offenses score points, but defenses win games. True in football, and true in managing retirement investments.

Even before I got into the business of retirement income planning, I knew that buying high and selling low was a bad idea. Now I know that eliminating loss from the picture altogether is an even better idea. This is done by using insurance-based products in sequences and eliminating the possibility of market-induced losses. This does, of course, limit some of your upside market gain potential. But after the hard knocks of the past few years, my friends, family and neighbors – as well as I – would choose safety and a reasonable rate of return over the possibility of double-digit market gains or losses. In other words, we're favoring defense over offense.

The Steelers organization offers us a valuable lesson about loss prevention: It doesn't make sense to risk your hard-earned principal to the market when you can win the game by being intelligently defensive. Do the math – literally!

Which would you prefer? A retirement lifestyle contingent on the whims of the market, or lifetime income you can rely on?

NEW MONEY LESSON

Defend against loss.

It doesn't make sense to put your blind trust in the markets (e.g., stocks, bonds and mutual funds) when you can rely on simple math and logic to create a lifetime of retirement income that can't be outlived.

Although this is the last chapter of the book, I hope it's not the end of your quest to achieve the best retirement possible. I congratulate you if, after reading the book, you feel compelled to take action toward creating and executing a game plan that's based on math and not reliant on the market. A plan to deliver:

- Safety of principal
- Reasonable rates of return
- Income that continues throughout your and your spouse's lives
- The peace of mind that comes with knowing you'll have a comfortable retirement lifestyle

So, the end of my book is hopefully a beginning for you to investigate your options and build a plan that makes sense to you. If you end up working with us at Bleier Zagula to formulate your plan, that's great. But if it's with someone else who gives you that same peace of mind, then my goal is still accomplished.

The economic environment today is just too shaky to go it alone. Build a solid team that you feel comfortable with, and you'll be on the right track to achieving your retirement aspirations.

The final lesson? TRUST YOURSELF.

As William Jennings Bryan said, "Destiny is not a matter of chance, it's a matter of choice; it's not a thing to be waited for, but it's a thing to be achieved. And each and every one of our destinies lies right in our own hands, where it can become what we want to it become."

Whether in football or in retirement planning, if you think you are beaten, you are. If you think you cannot, you don't. If you like to win and think you can't, it's almost a cinch you won't. Life's battles won't always go to the stronger or faster man, but sooner or later, the one who wins is the one who thinks he can.

And you're a winner.
God bless.

Printed in the USA
CPSIA information can be obtained
at www.ICGtesting.com
JSHW062053050624
64351JS00013B/123/J